ECOLOGY WATCH

TOWNS AND CITIES

Rodney Aldis

93-9600

DILLON PRESS
NEW YORK

First American publication 1992 by Dillon Press, Macmillan Publishing Company, 866 Third Avenue, New York, NY 10022

Macmillan Publishing Company is part of the Maxwell Communication Group of Companies

First published by Evans Brothers Limited, 2A Portman Mansions, Chiltern Street, London W1M 1LE.

Typeset by Fleetlines Typesetters, Southend-on-Sea
Printed in Spain by GRAFO, S.A.—Bilbao

10 9 8 7 6 5 4 3 2 1
Aldis, Rodney.
     Towns and cities / Rodney Aldis.
        p. cm. — (Ecology watch)
     Includes index.
     Summary: Examines urban plants and animals, their survival techniques in the city, and methods of keeping them from being endangered.
        ISBN 0-87518-496-0
        1. Urban ecology (Biology)—Juvenile literature. [1. Urban animals. 2. Urban plants. 3. Urban ecology (Biology) 4. Ecology.]
     I. Title. II. Series.
     QH541.5.C6A43 1992
     574.5'268—dc20   91-35801

Acknowledgments

Editor: Su Swallow
Design: Neil Sayer
Production: Jenny Mulvanny

Illustrations: David Gardner, Graeme Chambers
Diagram p.11: Hardlines, Charlbury

For permission to reproduce copyright material the author and publishers gratefully acknowledge the following:

Cover (London) G. I. Bernard, NHPA
Title page (Rosebay willowherb) Dr Eckart Pott, Bruce Coleman Limited

p4 Fritz Prenzel, Bruce Coleman Limited **p5** (inset, top) Martyn Chillmain, Oxford Scientific Films, (inset, bottom) Terry Heathcote, Oxford Scientific Films **p6** Keith Kent, Science Photo Library **p7** (top) Mike Birkhead, Oxford Scientific Films, (bottom) Hattie Young, Science Photo Library **p8** Hans Reinhard, Bruce Coleman Limited **p9** E. A. Janes, NHPA **p10** Barbara C. Harrison, Oxford Scientific Films **p12** (left) Jane Burton, Bruce Coleman Limited, (right) Hans Reinhard, Bruce Coleman Limited **p13** John Cancalosi , Bruce Coleman Limited **p14** Nicholas de Vore, Bruce Coleman Limited **p15** (top) Brian Hawkes, NHPA, (bottom left) Hans Reinhard, Bruce Coleman Limited, (bottom right) Okapia/Oxford Scientific Films **p16** Kim Taylor, Bruce Coleman Limited **p17** (top) George McCarthy, Bruce Coleman Limited, (bottom) Kim Taylor, Bruce Coleman Limited **p18** M. P. L. Fogden, Bruce Coleman Limited **p19** C. B. and D. W. Frith, Bruce Coleman Limited **p20** Mary Evans Picture Library **p21** Fritz Prenzel, Bruce Coleman Limited **p22** Mike Birkhead, Oxford Scientific Films **p23** (top) Hermann Brehm, Bruce Coleman Limited, (bottom) P. and W. Ward, Oxford Scientific Films **p24** Sally Morgan/ECOSCENE **p25** Adrian Davies, Bruce Coleman Limited, (inset) Meech/ECOSCENE **p26** P. Evans, Bruce Coleman Limited **p27** Greenwood/ECOSCENE **p28** (top) Mike Birkhead, Oxford Scientific Films, (bottom) Anna Walsh, Oxford Scientific Films **p29** (top) Sally Morgan/ECOSCENE, (bottom) Roger Wilmshurst, Bruce Coleman Limited **p30** Jan Van de Kam, Bruce Coleman Limited **p31** (top) David Nicholls/ECOSCENE **p32** (top) Michael P. Price, Bruce Coleman Limited, (bottom) Norbert Rosing, Bruce Coleman Limited **p33** Jane Burton, Bruce Coleman Limited **p34** David Woodfall, NHPA **p35** Hans Reinhard, Bruce Coleman Limited **p36** (top) Uwe Walz, Bruce Coleman Limited, (bottom) Sally Morgan/ECOSCENE **p37** David Woodfall, NHPA **p38** (top) Laurie Campbell, NHPA, (bottom) Leonard Lee Rue, Bruce Coleman Limited **p39** (top) Nigel Dennis, NHPA, (bottom) Terry Heathcote, Oxford Scientific Films **p40** Sally Morgan/ECOSCENE **p41** Eric Crichton, Bruce Coleman Limited, (inset) Michael Rose, Frank Lane Picture Agency **p42** Fritz Prenzel, Bruce Coleman Limited **p43** (top) C. James, Bruce Coleman Limited, (bottom) Gerald Cubitt, Bruce Coleman Limited **p44** (top) Greenwood/ECOSCENE, (bottom) Mike Birkhead, Oxford Scientific Films.

Contents

Introduction

Towns and cities are found on every continent except Antarctica and in every major type of landscape. They are new environments for people and wildlife—the first towns did not appear until about 9,000 years ago. Most cities are located on the boundary between two different environments, for example where mountain foothills meet open plains or where land meets the sea. It is at these boundaries that opportunities are created for people to develop trade and industry.

We tend to think of the city and the countryside as being two completely different environments, the city as the environment for people and the countryside as the environment for wildlife. But farm fields sprayed each year with pesticides are usually less rich in wildlife than tree-lined city streets and leafy gardens. For some animals there is much more food in cities than in the countryside. This is why the **feral pigeon** is more numerous in European towns and cities than its wild relative, the rock dove, and the starling is more abundant in well-watered suburban yards than in **deciduous** woodlands.

Unfortunately, most cities are particularly attractive to the kinds of wildlife that are pests. Rats and mice, for example, thrive in human settlements, where they spoil food supplies and spread disease. Pigeons and starlings damage buildings with their droppings. The challenge, however, is to make our cities attractive to desirable kinds of wildlife rather than to those that are pests. To do that, we have to understand the **ecology** of cities and how they fit into the larger landscape, a landscape that includes a range of habitats from built-up areas to mountaintop wildernesses.

Wildlife in cities is important because it can teach us about the balance of nature. A danger of city living is that we become cut off from nature, and this affects our attitude

toward the natural world. Watching the comings and goings of wild animals and the seasonal changes in plants is also an enjoyable experience for many people. In a recent survey in Germany, most people said the reason they visited their local town parks was that they liked to see the wildlife. In the United States, where three quarters of the population live in towns and cities, over half the adults say they enjoy watching wildlife

Canberra, Australia (above) has been planned to encourage wildlife, but some plants and animals (insets: poppy and peacock butterfly) can survive in the most built-up areas of cities.

around their homes, and one in six keep bird feeders. Many have also set aside natural areas on their property for wildlife.

Words printed in **bold** are explained at the end of each section.

feral pigeon—wild pigeon found in towns, descended from domestic pigeons, which escaped from medieval dovecotes.

deciduous—describes trees that lose all their leaves each year.

ecology—the relationships between living organisms and their environment.

City climate

The climate of cities is slightly different from that of the countryside that surrounds them. The differences are not great but they do have some effects on city wildlife, and as cities expand the differences may affect the climate of whole regions. Cities are warmer, have a higher rainfall but lower **humidity**, lower wind speeds, and less fog than the surrounding countryside.

The nature of building materials affects the temperature of cities. Bricks, stone, concrete, and tarred surfaces absorb and store heat from the sun through the day. The hard surfaces act as a kind of heat bank. During the night the stored heat is radiated back to the air above. The warmed air expands and rises, and when this happens air rushes into the city center, creating strong gusts of wind. And as the air rises over the city center, thunderstorms are produced. The number of thunderstorms over cities is one and a half times more than in the countryside. The increase in thunderstorms causes cities to have up to one third more **precipitation** than the surrounding countryside. Cities also produce heat by using energy for heating, for air conditioning, and for vehicles. The heat released adds to the warming of cities.

Surprisingly, perhaps, only about two thirds of an urban area is covered by hard surfaces. One third of the city land surface is made up of roads and paths. Another third is

▽ More rain falls in the city than in the surrounding countryside.

6

△ In the winter, more than a million starlings may roost together.

taken up by buildings. About one third of the area is covered with grass, trees, shrubs, and other kinds of "semi-natural" vegetation.

Plants transfer heat to the air, but they do so mainly by evaporating water. When water evaporates, heat is stored in the water vapor and is not released into the air until the water vapor condenses. This usually happens more than a mile above the ground. Landscapes covered with vegetation, such as forests, therefore have a cooler, more humid climate than built-up areas.

Buildings in cities affect the flow of air. They increase the speed of strong winds, while light winds are slowed even further. Wind speeds are on average about one third less than they are in the countryside, and still air also helps to increase the temperature of cities.

The warmer climate of towns and cities is an attraction to many species of animals, particularly in those parts of the world where the winters are cold or windy. In Europe and North America large flocks of starlings spend the winter nights **roosting** on buildings and in trees close to many city centers.

The warmer temperatures mean that the growing season for plants is longer. Plants begin flowering earlier in the spring and bloom until later in the autumn. Insects become active earlier, especially those such as bees and butterflies that depend upon flowers to provide them with food.

Cities have a higher rainfall than the surrounding countryside, but they are similar in some ways to deserts. That is because rainwater drains off the hard surfaces of buildings and streets very quickly. Much of the water is piped into rivers and streams, leaving very little lying on the surface in pools. The lack of surface water makes it harder for some animals, such as frogs, to live in our towns and cities. Plants also suffer from a shortage of water.

Pollution problems

In the nineteenth century and first half of the twentieth century the air in some cities, particularly in Europe and parts of the United States, became very polluted. Many people became ill or died. In 1952 in London 4,000 people died in one week as a result of **smog**.

Gases from factories, power stations, vehicles, and oil- and coal-fired heating systems pollute the air and often form a

▽ Air pollution affects people and wildlife.

"haze cone" over large cities. Air pollution produces acid rain, which in some places kills plants and causes changes in the chemistry of soils and water. The increased rainfall over cities means that more pollutants are washed out of the air than in the countryside, and the pollutants that are washed down make soils and water more acid. It is harder for plants to absorb important **nutrients,** such as calcium and nitrates, when the soils and water are acid. But some plants are adapted to live in acid soils, so they have an advantage over other plants in cities affected by acid rain.

In some ways, the situation has improved since the 1950s, when clean air laws were passed in many countries. These laws control the burning of coal and have reduced significantly the pollution from particles of soot and dust. The cleaner air has led to increases in flying insects, which in turn have brought insect-feeding birds such as swifts and swallows back to towns and cities.

However, the increase in the numbers of cars has led to an increase in pollution from internal combustion engines. The problem is most severe in cities that are located in basins hemmed in by mountains and with warm, sunny climates, such as Los Angeles, California, and Sydney, Australia. Strong sunlight causes the chemicals in car exhaust fumes to change into a dangerous photochemical smog. In Los Angeles, air pollution levels are sometimes so high that it is dangerous for people to be outdoors.

Looking at lichens

Some plants, for example **conifers** and **lichens**, are particularly affected by air pollution and do not live well in most cities. In fact, lichens can be used as indicators of changes in the cleanness of the air. If lichens are found to be spreading then we can be reasonably sure the quality of air is improving, and vice versa. Some lichen species, however, have actually benefited from air pollution. Large lichens usually crowd out small, fast-growing ones but where the air pollution is high, it usually prevents the large lichens from growing.

◁ A swallow brings insects for its young.

▽ Lichens grow well in clean air.

Some small lichens have spread as competition from the large ones has decreased.

Color change

Some kinds of animals have adapted very rapidly to the changes that air pollution has caused to the environment. One striking example is that of peppered moths. In areas unaffected by soot these moths are light colored. In their natural environment the trees have bark usually covered in lichens, which have a light color. In industrial areas the tree bark lichens are killed, and the bark is covered with a dark layer of soot. The light moths are easily seen by insect-eating birds when they sit on dark tree trunks, and they are soon eaten. In the past, this meant that only the darker moths were left to breed, and within 50 years dark-colored peppered moths had almost completely replaced the light-colored ones in industrial regions. Elsewhere the light-colored ones were still the most common. Now that the amounts of soot have decreased, the light-colored peppered moths are becoming more common in industrial regions once again. Similar adaptations to dark surfaces caused by air pollution have been found in other small animals, too. The zebra spider, for example, is normally striped in black and white, but in industrial regions it is entirely black.

humidity—describes the amount of moisture in the air.
precipitation—moisture that falls as rain, snow, sleet, etc.
roosting—(of birds) resting or sleeping on a perch, branch etc.
smog— a combination of smoke, fog and chemical fumes.
nutrients—chemicals absorbed by plants for nourishment.
conifers—trees that bear cones and evergreen leaves (usually needlelike).
lichens—a group of plants composed of a fungus and an alga growing together.

The pattern of cities

Until the turn of the twentieth century, cities were built-up islands set in the expanse of the countryside, but as this century has progressed cities have tended to grow until many of them have joined up with their neighbors. Over large areas of Europe, North America, and parts of Asia there is no longer a clear boundary between cities and the countryside but rather a mix of suburbs, farm fields and woods. This is an advantage to those kinds of wildlife that get much of their food from humans or that can live in small areas of habitat. It is a disadvantage to those such as brown bears that need large areas of natural, undisturbed habitat.

The urban patchwork

A city is a patchwork of habitats, from parks, ponds, and vacant lots to buildings, roads, and athletic fields. As a general rule the variety of wild plants and animals decreases as we move toward the city center. However, this is only because there is usually less vegetation toward the center. In those cities that have pockets of woods and parks close to the center, the variety of wildlife is sometimes surprisingly high.

There is a pattern to the way most cities are built and in the way the patchwork of habitats is arranged. The pattern has been decided by the laws of economics rather than the laws of nature. The most valuable land is in the city centers and that is where the main government buildings, large offices and stores are located. Around the center are the suburbs in which most people live.

The lie of the land does have some effects on the city pattern. The southern part of London, for example, has grown along the outlying valleys, leaving many of the ridges clothed in woodland and heath. Los Angeles, in southern California, has grown along ridges that are separated by deep, brush-filled gullies that are too narrow and steep to build on. The gullies allow coyotes to live deep in the suburbs, where residents can hear them howling at night.

Land in the city center is more expensive than that farther out, so it is there that we find many tall buildings packed together. For wildlife, the center of a city is a habitat of cliffs, ledges, and rock surfaces rather like rocky mountaintops. Just as some birds nest on cliffs and mountaintops, birds such as pigeons and falcons nest on tall buildings.

As we move away from the center the price of land drops. Multistory office buildings give way to houses, and with houses we begin to find lawns, tree-lined streets, and public parks. For wildlife the stony cliff habitat is gradually replaced by small areas of grassland and open woodland. The farther we move from the center the larger the green areas and parks become. The variety of wild animals increases as the area of land covered with grasses, shrubs, and trees increases.

The town pigeons of the stony city center

▽ Coyote

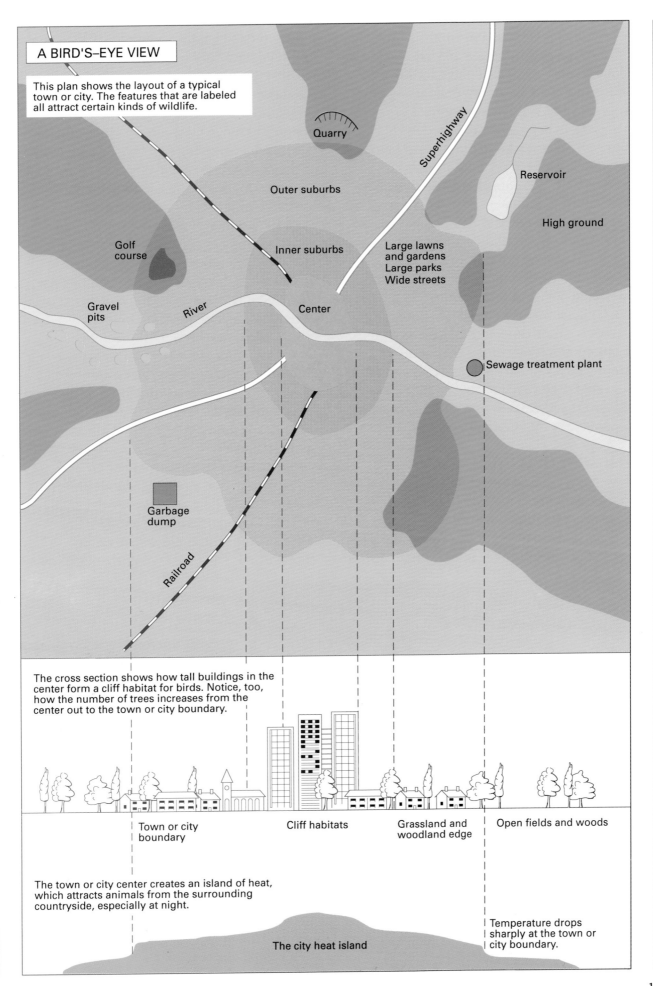

A BIRD'S-EYE VIEW

This plan shows the layout of a typical town or city. The features that are labeled all attract certain kinds of wildlife.

Quarry

Outer suburbs

Superhighway

Reservoir

High ground

Golf course

Inner suburbs

Large lawns and gardens
Large parks
Wide streets

Gravel pits

River

Center

Sewage treatment plant

Garbage dump

Railroad

The cross section shows how tall buildings in the center form a cliff habitat for birds. Notice, too, how the number of trees increases from the center out to the town or city boundary.

Town or city boundary

Cliff habitats

Grassland and woodland edge

Open fields and woods

The town or city center creates an island of heat, which attracts animals from the surrounding countryside, especially at night.

Temperature drops sharply at the town or city boundary.

The city heat island

are replaced in the suburbs by woodland birds such as woodpeckers. Woodland animals such as squirrels scurry along the branches of trees, and in tropical cities we may see monkeys (see page 39). In tall trees in old gardens and along streets even large birds are able to find secluded places to nest out of sight of passersby. Some suburban properties have a rich variety of habitats. There are lawns (which are like grasslands), patches of shrubs (shrub woodland), taller trees (woodland), and ponds.

Traveling farther outward we eventually reach the open countryside beyond the city. We could stop our safari at this boundary between suburb and countryside, but there is still more we can find if we continue. Among the boundary habitats that attract wildlife are sewage treatment plants, reservoirs, gravel pits, and garbage dumps, separated by transportation routes.

Wildlife in a line

If we move around the edge of the city we may have to cross railroad lines and highways radiating out from the city to various parts of the country. These communications routes are also habitats for many kinds of wildlife. Railroad embankments and highway verges are hardly ever visited by people, and many plants and animals live there almost undisturbed. The verges also allow wild animals to move between the cities and the countryside, carrying plant seeds with them as they go. A river or canal may cut through the city, too, providing a habitat for many freshwater plants and animals.

Road and railroad verges provide long narrow strips of grassy and shrubby habitat. These are often our new unofficial nature reserves. Highway verges, for example, are good habitat for grass-eating animals such as field mice, and these are hunted by hawks, which are frequently seen hovering above the traffic. In many places highway embankments are planted with shrubs and small trees. Such areas provide a shrub woodland habitat for insects, insect-eating birds, foxes, and birds of prey such as sparrow hawks.

Railroad embankments are often overgrown with a thicket of woody shrubs and brambles. Pedestrians are not usually allowed to walk there, so except for the noise of trains these places are often undisturbed. The lack of disturbance allows

◁ Gray squirrel
▽ Sparrow hawk

Plants beside the highway

When a new highway is built, the verge is sown with grasses such as rye, red fescue and meadow grass. These, and other plants such as clover, hold down the soil and prevent soil erosion.

Other plants such as vetches, campions, dandelions, cowslips and buttercups gradually invade the grassland. The seeds are carried there by the wind and by animals.

Later, shrubs such as blackthorn, bramble, dog rose, elder and gorse appear. Trees such as ash, oak and sycamore eventually develop. The lower slope of the verge may be mown occasionally to prevent trees from growing too close to the highway.

plants to grow that in other parts of the city are trampled or collected. Although many kinds of wildlife benefit from these transportation routes, some species are disadvantaged. Highways and electrified railroad lines divide the country into blocks of land. Large animals, such as deer and bears, may find it difficult to cross these barriers. The motor vehicle is for many animals their most dangerous enemy. The habitats of large animals are fragmented by roads and railroad lines, and this can lead to the disappearance of species from their habitats. However, some animals learn to use tunnels or underpasses beneath busy roads. Underpasses have been built in England for badgers and in Australia for wombats.

▽ Hairy-nosed wombat

13

City cliffs and caves

In the city center

The most obvious difference between city and country is in the number of buildings, but to animals and plants the walls and roof spaces of buildings are much the same as cliffs and caves. The ledges and roofs of tall buildings provide resting and nesting places for birds that naturally live in rocky and mountainous country. Sea gulls, for example, are becoming used to living in the centers of cities. To a sea gull the ledges and roofs of buildings are much the same as the rocky sea cliffs as places to make their nests. The peregrine falcon, a large bird of prey, is normally associated with wild mountains and wilderness areas, but it, too, is beginning to colonize some cities. There is a well-known colony in Toronto, Canada, for example. The peregrine falcon catches birds by swooping at them while they are in flight. In cities peregrines use tall buildings as lookout posts to watch for flying birds.

Heavy industrial areas may look ugly and uninviting to people, but they provide many nesting opportunities for hole-nesting birds. Birds such as pigeons, crows, and ospreys use the spaces in the metal frameworks of power stations, electricity pylons, railroad station buildings, and warehouses.

Plant power

It is not only animals that use a city's artificial cliffs, ledges, and other hard surfaces. Walls, paving stones, even limestone memorials, provide the right

▽ New York City in the winter

14

Town birds

Pigeon power

Small numbers of the wild rock dove live around the coasts of Britain, southern Europe, and northern Africa, where they nest in crevices and caves among rocks. The town pigeon, which is related to the wild rock dove, lives in large groups and nests on buildings. The wild bird eats mostly seeds, buds, and leaves but the town pigeon eats whatever is available. It is an opportunist, searching the streets and public squares for tidbits, and raiding dockside warehouses where grain is stored.

Pigeons are known to carry parrot disease, which can be passed to people, and which affects the lungs. Sandboxes in playgrounds can become infected with this disease if they are fouled by pigeons. Because town pigeons have reliable supplies of food, it is possible for diseased pigeons to survive longer than they do in the countryside, where life is harder. The peregrine falcon is the natural predator of

△ Rooks nesting at an oil refinery

kind of surface (an alkaline one) for several kinds of plants, especially lichens. In one study in Cambridge, England, 186 species of plants were found growing on walls. However, air pollution in city centers and industrial areas may be too great for most kinds of lichens. Lichens are usually the first plants to colonize bare rocky surfaces. They prepare the ground for more complex and more demanding plants, such as mosses, ferns, and herbs (see pages 9 and 22). Without the lichens, the artificial surfaces often remain bare.

△ Pigeons in Cracow, Poland

◁ Peregrine falcon

15

pigeons, and the low numbers of these birds in cities also mean the pigeons are not greatly hunted. However, with the increase in falcons in some cities, life for town pigeons may not be as safe as it once was.

Pigeon droppings are a problem on buildings where they rest. The birds also peck at the mortar between the bricks to get the lime (for the minerals it contains), and that can speed up the decay of buildings. Sometimes it is necessary to control their numbers when natural predators are absent.

Super starling

The European starling is naturally a bird of the woodland edge, feeding in grasslands and resting and nesting in tall trees. As the natural forests have been cleared, so the starling has moved westward from its original home on the grasslands of eastern Europe. It has been introduced to North America, Australia, and New Zealand, where it has proved to be very successful. In fact, about 200 million starlings—about one third of the world's population—live in North America. They are all descended from 100 birds that were introduced into Central Park in New York in the late nineteenth century (see page 37).

The starling is successful because it is so adaptable. It is able to feed in backyards, woodlands, farms, and city parks. The birds gather together in flocks to feed and roost. In cities, they roost in street trees and on ledges on buildings that provide shelter from the wind. All small birds, including starlings, must burn food to supply their bodies with heat if the air temperature drops below 60°F. The stronger the winds the more food they must burn. As average wind speeds are less in cities than they are in the countryside and the temperatures are higher, starlings have gained by roosting in cities.

The starling has its good and bad points as far as humans are concerned. In the spring the birds benefit farmers by eating large numbers of the tough-skinned larvae of crane flies, which are a serious pest of grasses. To fruit growers, however, starlings are a nuisance when cherries and other fruits are ripening. In towns and cities, their

△ A male starling sings from his nest site.

droppings can create a lot of mess and spread certain diseases.

In the suburbs

City suburbs suit three main groups of wild animals: those that can make use of houses as a habitat; those that live along the edges of woodland (see page 34); and those that feed at the woodland edge but use cliffs or caves as nesting and resting places. Trees in suburban parks and yards serve as the woodland edge, while houses provide animals with cliff and cave habitats. House walls are "cliffs," and the cavity between the roof and the ceiling is a "cave."

On the house wall

One of the most numerous birds in cities is the house sparrow, which over the past 100 years has doubled the area it inhabits and now inhabits one quarter of the earth's land surface. The house sparrow is a seed-eating bird, a member of the finch family. It thrives on derelict land where the colonizing plants produce large quantities of seeds (see page 22). It also makes use of the food put on bird feeders and scraps dropped in streets. It

△ The house martin has a white rump, which helps to distinguish it from the swallow.

▽ Pipistrelle bats and (below) long-eared bats often roost in buildings.

usually builds its untidy nest of dry grass on or in houses, under the eaves and beneath roof tiles. Both parents feed the young, which hatch after about two weeks, and which can fly about two weeks later.

The house martin is a summer visitor to Europe where it breeds. In Europe it has become associated with people because it depends upon the walls of buildings to make its nest, which is an elaborate structure made of mud. It spends the winter south of the African Sahara. House martins, like swifts and swallows, feed on flying insects.

Moving into the roof space

Bats on the wing

In urban areas, bats are most common where there are areas of open space such as parks and waterways, for the insects on which they feed are much more common in these habitats than over built-up areas. Because bats can fly they are able to travel easily around cities in search of food and roosting sites. They hunt in the late evening and during the night, feeding on flying insects. They have evolved a system of reflected sound, similar to sonar, to detect insects. Their **echolocation** system also allows them to avoid obstacles such as overhead wires, pylons, and buildings.

Worldwide there are about 980 species of bats, of which 30 live in Europe. The smallest and most common bat in Europe is the pipistrelle, which has adapted easily to life in the city. It is usually found in buildings, where it roosts in the roof space. In the summer the females congregate in large roosts of up to 700 individuals. Each female gives birth in June to a single baby. Young bats can fend for themselves after about six weeks. At the approach of winter, when the numbers of insects on which they feed fall, pipistrelle bats go into hibernation until the following spring.

Raccoons in the garbage

The raccoon is found in North and Central America, although it is related to the giant panda of Asia. The raccoon naturally uses a tree hollow or a small cave as its dwelling. It eats a wide variety of foods and in the countryside usually hunts along streams and around marshes. However, it has taken to life in the suburbs easily, too well for some people. Many North American suburbs are spacious; houses with large yards and plenty of trees and shrubs allow raccoons to forage for food. Raccoons also scavenge for food scraps in garbage cans and outside hotel and restaurant kitchens. They often make such a mess by scavenging that garbage cans have to be raccoon-proof.

The cavity between roof and ceiling is a fine replacement for a hole in a tree, where the female raccoon can give birth to her young. Raccoons have also been known to raise their babies in chimneys, which can cause the youngsters problems when the time comes to leave home. Many chimneys are tall and it is a long drop for a young raccoon just out of its family's den.

A marsupial mammal
Opossums are found from Argentina to the northern United States. (There are several related "'possum" in Australia and New Guinea.) Opossums usually make their homes in tree hollows but where none is available, they will happily use any suitable dark hole. Like the raccoon, the 'possum often makes its home in the roof spaces of houses, particularly the older weatherboard ones and those that are surrounded by mature trees, which allow the animals to come and go easily. The opossum is about as big as a domestic cat and can squeeze into small gaps in the wall or roof, moving loose bricks or tiles aside where necessary. The female gives birth to a single baby once or twice a year. The opossum is a **marsupial mammal**: The baby lives in its mother's pouch for four or five months while it develops; then it rides on its mother's back for another two months until it is weaned.

Opossums can be quite noisy and may fight to defend or take over a nest site. Often the only way to get rid of a 'possum living in a roof space is to block every possible entry hole at night while the animal is out feeding.

Opossum

◁ Raccoons raid a garbage can.

△ The carpet python and other snakes feed on rats and mice.

Unwelcome house guests

The increase of trade and the movement of people since the Middle Ages have allowed many animals (and plants) to spread beyond their natural home ranges. The heating of buildings whether by fires or central heating allows many tropical animals to live in cooler regions. Buildings suit animals that live or hide in cracks, crevices, and small holes. Some of these animals are harmless while others, such as the brown rat and house mouse, are responsible for a great deal of damage to buildings and human food supplies and may also carry diseases. Termites and death watch and long-horned beetles eat wood, which can cause buildings to collapse.

Of rats, mice, and snakes

Some of the most undesirable creatures in built-up areas are brown rats, black rats, and house mice. A study of rats in one American city estimated that there were about 160,000 rats in the city, with about 150 in the average inner-city apartment building. Rat popu-lations are much higher in many developing countries. In cities in India, for example, there are about six rats for every person.

Rats and mice are able to breed very rapidly and produce three or more litters a year, with up to ten young in each. They spoil food supplies, damage buildings by eating through wood, plastic, and rubber, and carry diseases. Unfortunately, birds of prey, cats, foxes, and other predators are not able to keep the numbers of rats and mice low enough for our health needs. Often the only way to control them is to lay out poison, although the effect does not last long.

Some snakes are useful predators. In Australia and New Guinea, carpet pythons are long slender snakes that eat rodents and other small animals. People sometimes encourage these snakes to live in their roof cavities because they are one way of controlling unwelcome visitors such as rats, mice, and house-nesting birds. In other parts of the world cobras and rat snakes are often found in human settlements, where they, too, live off the rich supply of rats and mice.

Insect pests and parasites

The human flea is a **parasite** mainly of mammals that live in holes, so it probably became adapted to living on humans when our ancestors lived in caves. The rat flea feeds on the blood of the black rat and will also bite people. It is responsible for carrying the **bubonic plague** from black rats to humans. In Europe in the Middle Ages outbreaks of bubonic plague killed millions of people. In the fourteenth century a major epidemic reduced the population of Europe by one quarter. Bubonic plague became rare in Europe as the brown rat arrived and replaced the black rat as a common resident of houses. The brown rat is less likely to carry bubonic plague, so this change in wildlife removed a major health threat to people living in Europe.

Cats and dogs also carry fleas. Cat fleas seem to prefer the environment inside houses more than dog fleas. Dog fleas are more likely to be found on dogs in outside kennels than on dogs that live indoors. Both kinds of fleas will bite humans if they are hungry enough.

▽ A victim of bubonic plague in 1665

Danger—termites at work

Termites are insects that are found in warm regions of the world. They feed on the cellulose in wood and grass. In the countryside termites perform a very important job by breaking down plant matter such as wood and dead leaves and by releasing the nutrients that are bound up in it. Their job is especially important in regions where the climate is too dry for soil bacteria to thrive. However, in towns and cities termites are a problem, particularly in houses with wooden frames and beams. Some unfortunate house owners have realized too late that while they were sleeping, termites were busily chewing away at their houses. Whole houses can collapse after being attacked by termites.

Spiders

Spiders are predators, mainly of insects and other **arthropods.** Most spider species are creatures of warm, dry climates. However, the warmth of buildings has allowed several species to thrive in colder parts of the world such as northern Europe and Canada. There are two major groups of spiders: those that make webs in which their prey becomes trapped and those that hunt. All spiders digest their food by injecting digestive juices into the bodies of their victims. They then drink the liquid that is produced.

The house spider makes a "sheet net" web, often across the corner of a window. The spitting spider, with its distinctive yellow body and black spots, traps its prey by squirting sticky threads over its victim. Some spiders produce very powerful venoms. One of the most dangerous spiders is the Sydney funnel web spider, which is related to the large bird-eating spider of South America. The funnel web spider makes a burrow that is protected at the entrance by a silken funnel. The burrows are made in the dry sandy soils found above the sandstone rocks of north Sydney, Australia. In Australia many houses are built on low piers, and the spiders make their holes in the ground beneath the floors. Children are warned not to play beneath houses because of the danger of being bitten by funnel web

△ A funnel web spider ready to strike

spiders. The venom is extremely poisonous, and unless victims are treated quickly with an antivenin death is very likely. The poison affects the nervous system, and the victim's lungs fill with liquid.

Another Australian spider, the red-back spider, is related to the American black widow spider. It is often found in sheds and outbuildings and even under toilet seats. Its venom can be extremely painful and is sometimes fatal, particularly to young children. However, the chance of death from a dangerous spider even in Australia and the United States is about the same as being struck by lightning. Most kinds of spiders are harmless to people. Even if some species do bite, the effect is—with a few exceptions—only a minor irritation.

echolocation—a system of finding out where objects are by measuring the time it takes for an echo to return from them.

marsupial—relating to any mammal that continues to develop in its mother's pouch after birth.

mammal—warm-blooded animal that feeds on its mother's milk after birth.

parasite—a plant or animal that lives and feeds on another.

bubonic plague—an infectious disease giving rise to fever and swellings, caused by a rat flea bite.

arthropods—a group of animals with jointed limbs, segmented body, and outside skeleton, including insects, spiders, and crustaceans.

Wastelands

Nature takes over

The use of land changes as economic conditions change. When people run out of land to grow food, forests are cleared to provide more farmland. When more houses are needed, farmland may give way to houses. Each time the use of land changes, so do the habitats for wild plants and animals. Sometimes, when people have no further use for an area of land, it becomes derelict. Many cities have large amounts of derelict land. The reasons are many: factories close and are not redeveloped; people move away from the inner cities, leaving vacant properties; and so on.

When land is abandoned and becomes derelict, it provides opportunities for wild plants and animals. It is on wasteland that we can see the resilience of nature and its powers to heal the scars left by human activities. For wild plants and animals, derelict land means starting anew, much in the way that life starts again on volcanic lava flows or on land exposed by retreating glaciers and ice sheets.

Derelict land is an ideal habitat for the rapid colonizers, the plants adapted to take advantage of disturbed land, of new bare surfaces. Brick and stone walls provide opportunities for plants usually found in dry, rocky environments. Walls and sidewalks favor plants able to cope with dry conditions, because one of the features of

▽ Coltsfoot grows on bare and waste ground. Its bright flowers appear before the leaves.

△ Goldfinches enjoy feeding on thistles.

▽ Cinnabar moth caterpillars feed on ragwort.

these habitats is that rainwater drains away very quickly. On sidewalks the best places for plants are the gaps between the cement slabs, where water collects. Mortar and cement, which bind the bricks and stones of walls together, are rich in calcium carbonate. Where this begins to dissolve, plants such as rusty black fern, shepherd's purse, and common mouse-ear chickweed, which are adapted to live in lime-rich soils, thrive.

On open derelict land we will probably find many different grasses and plants such as wild asters and daisies. Once plants become established they provide shelter and food for plant-eating animals, which in turn attract predators, and food chains soon develop. One of the features of colonizing flowering plants is the great amount of seed they produce that attracts seed-eating animals such as mice, sparrows, and goldfinches. The seed-eating animals in turn attract predators such as owls, hawks, and foxes. In time larger plants may invade derelict sites. Shrubs and trees increase the number of plant layers, increasing the opportunities for more kinds of animals.

The new wilderness

Derelict areas can be very rich in wild plants and animals, and they have an advantage in that they are cheap to maintain—they do not need anyone to tend them! One of the best examples is the old site of the Anhatter and Potsdam Railroad Station in Berlin, Germany. The station was bombed in World War II and an area of 170 acres was left derelict for many years afterward. A large number of plant species, about one third of all the species that grow in the Berlin area, are found on the site. They include more than 100 species of trees and more than 300 species of grasses, herbs, mosses, and ferns, including 17 endangered species. Only a few of the trees are native to the area. The rest are non-native trees that have spread from streets and parks.

In many cities around the world derelict land has been used to create natural parks, which people enjoy visiting. London, like all major cities, has many derelict sites, but some of these have been taken over by community groups and turned into nature parks. One such area is near a main line railroad station. In 1066 the area around what is now called Camley Street, near King's Cross railroad station in north London, was mostly deciduous forest. As London expanded, the forest was cleared to make way for farms. In the 1820s a canal was opened, and trade in the area increased. The coal business increased with the building of the railroads and by the 1870s Camley Street was a storage area for coal. However, the use of coal declined in the 1950s, and the site became an unofficial waste dump. Today, it is a thriving nature park.

Although the park is only about two and one-half acres, it has a large pond, meadows, and a small woodland. These habitats have been created to provide a natural environment for birds, insects, frogs, and toads as well as a rich variety of plant life. The energy and determination of local people to improve their environment has created a park, which is now used by many schoolchildren every year for studies of wildlife and conservation. The park has been featured in television documentaries shown in several European countries.

However, the park is now under threat. The building of the Channel Tunnel has created a need for a new railroad terminal in London, and the park is sited in the area most favored by the developers. Now a new use for the area has arisen. What is the solution to this kind of problem? Is the answer to say nature comes first and the developers must find another site? Or is the answer to move the park, perhaps at the developers' expense?

▷ Reed beds and marsh plants in the Camley Street Natural Park provide nesting sites for birds, while the meadow flowers (inset) attract insects.

The butterfly bush

Buddleia is a flowering shrub native to China. It was introduced into Europe and North America as a garden plant toward the end of the nineteenth century. It is an easy shrub to grow and has escaped from gardens to grow wild in many places, and it is common on wasteland. The flowers attract nectar-seeking insects, particularly flower flies, bees, and butterflies, hence the plant's common name, the butterfly bush.

The leaves of the butterfly bush are eaten by the larvae of some small moths. The larvae are eaten by many kinds of insect-eating birds such as blue tits and robins. Sap-sucking insects, such as aphids, also feed on the leaves, and the aphids are hunted by ladybugs. These little beetles fly from tree to tree, often flying high in the air where some of them fall prey to swifts, which hunt insects on the wing. The butterfly bush therefore supports a whole community of animals.

25

Watery habitats

Rivers, ponds, and lakes greatly increase the variety of wildlife in cities. Some areas of water have been drained to provide land for building or for farming or for health reasons. In tropical countries, for example, swamps and stagnant water are drained because they are breeding grounds for malaria-carrying mosquitoes. In many places however, reservoirs, gravel pits, canals, and other artificial areas of water compensate to some extent for the loss of more natural watery habitats.

Rivers and canals

Rivers, like roadside and railroad verges, are corridor habitats cutting across the country. Seeds and animals may be carried into cities by the flow of water, while pollutants produced in cities may affect wildlife downstream.

Many cities are located on rivers or where rivers reach the sea. Rivers provide towns

▽ The still water of a canal

△ Mudflats on the Mersey River, England

and cities with reliable supplies of water both for drinking and for industrial uses. Major rivers, such as the Rhine and Mississippi, can be used by barges and ships for the carrying of freight and sometimes passengers. Besides being corridors for trade, rivers are also barriers, so many towns have grown up at points where rivers can be crossed easily.

Rivers increase the variety of wildlife living in cities. However, the types of wildlife will depend very much on the kind of river. Fast-flowing rivers in mountain regions will have a very different kind of wildlife from those slowly winding their way across low-lying plains. Most of the plant life is found where the rivers flow slowly.

The riverbank is also very important as a corridor for wildlife. Many insects and birds live in the vegetation that grows beside rivers. Herons and kingfishers feed on fish in the river, while others such as warblers hunt for insects living in the trees.

Canals resemble ponds rather than rivers as a wildlife habitat. Locks are used to hold water back, and it is only when the lock gates are opened that there is any noticeable flow of water. Canal beds are much more uniform than those of rivers and the water level changes very little. Most canals have banks and the oldest ones have a towpath along which horses and mules walked as they towed the canal boats with their cargoes. Like the riverbank the canal bank is also a wildlife corridor linking together widely separated habitats. Plants that grow on the bank and along the towpath include reeds, rushes, sedges, and nettles. The reed bunting may nest by the water, and the kingfisher dives in to catch fish. In Europe, canal fish range from tiny minnows to tench, bream, and pike. In cities where the canals are major traffic routes, the amount of wildlife is reduced, although the canals in Amsterdam attract large numbers of waterfowl, such as ducks and coots.

Canals that were built in the early years of the Industrial Revolution are usually too narrow to allow the passage of modern cargo barges. In Britain most canals are now obsolete except for use by pleasure craft, but this new use is a reason for maintaining them. Where canals are left to deteriorate, they gradually fill with water plants. The water level drops, and eventually trees and shrubs invade the bed until the watery habitats disappear altogether. The fate of canals is a good example of how economic changes affect the way land is used.

Salt marshes and mud flats

Many large cities—Rotterdam, Melbourne, and San Francisco, for example—are found on seacoasts, where salt marshes and mud flats are found in bays and river estuaries. These habitats are particularly rich feeding grounds for wading birds. Invertebrates such as lugworms and razor clams live in the mud, feeding on food brought in on the tide. As the tide goes out wading birds such as knots, dunlin, sandpipers, godwits, and curlews methodically search the exposed mud for invertebrates. Each species of wader is adapted to feed at different depths. In London large numbers of wading birds may be seen feeding on the mud flats at low tide on the Thames River and there are similar areas in many cities around the world.

Artificial lakes

Reservoirs

As towns and cities have grown it has become necessary to store drinking water. Reservoirs are artificial storage areas for water. Many cities have reservoirs located either in the city or on its fringes. These reservoirs are often on fertile soil, so the water is rich in the nutrients that water plants need. As wildlife habitats, reservoirs are similar to natural lakes. In some ways they are better because the changing water levels caused by water being drained off expose parts of the bed to the air, making water insects and plants more available to waterfowl and wading birds. In northwestern Europe and North America reservoirs are winter habitats for large flocks of migratory waterfowl such as Canada geese and wild ducks.

Gravel pits

All growing modern cities require concrete to construct buildings and roads. Large quantities of sand and gravel are needed to make concrete. These are heavy materials that are costly to transport over long distances, so builders like to obtain their supplies of sand and gravel as close to their city work sites as possible. The best sources of sand and gravel are the floodplains beside rivers, where the rivers have deposited these materials over many years. Once work stops, most pits become filled with water quite quickly. They then provide an ideal habitat for water birds such as swans, ducks, geese, and grebes. Migrating water birds follow rivers and find gravel pits easily.

▽ Sand martins (below) often nest in colonies in gravel pits (bottom) once the site is abandoned.

△ Restored gravel pits can be rich in wildlife (inset: bulrushes).

Common lizard

Gravel pits also provide habitat features that may not be common in the surrounding countryside. Sand martins make their nests in the pit sides, and lizards bask in the sun on mounds of sand and gravel. The little ringed plover, which breeds on pebbled shores, is now a common summer visitor to gravel pits in western Europe. The water plants that grow nearby support invertebrates on which the ringed plover feeds.

In time plants colonize the edges and shallows of the pits. Some of these plants, such as sea asters and saltbushes, are usually seen only on coastal sand dunes or in deserts.

The value of gravel pits has not been lost on naturalists and those with an interest in waterfowl. In Britain 3,700 acres of land are excavated each year to provide building materials, but three quarters of these are eventually flooded and landscaped into artificial lakes. Landscaping and planting can improve the habitat for wildlife much faster than leaving it to nature.

In Kent, England, a nature reserve has been developed around a gravel pit that has become a model for wildlife experts around the world. The gravel pit is on the edge of the town of Sevenoaks. Gravel taken from the pit was used to make the concrete for buildings that were put up in the 1960s in the town.

The edges of the pit were landscaped to create bays and shallow areas, which are preferred by some kinds of ducks for feeding. The shoreline and peninsulas were planted with trees and shrubs such as alder and willow. These provide cover, insects, and seeds for many small birds. Birch seeds fall into the water, where they are eaten by ducks. Artificial floating islands have been built where geese and terns are able to nest and the ducks can keep safe during the day, away from land-based predators such as foxes.

The reserve has been spectacularly successful in attracting wildlife. In 15 years the number of waterfowl increased by 500 percent. Of the smaller birds the sand martin is the most successful, and the increase is due to nesting habitat available in the "cliffs" of the gravel pit and to the increase in the number and variety of insects because of the planting that has taken place.

Sewage treatment plants

A very different kind of watery habitat is the sewage treatment plant. People can live safely, free from disease, in large numbers only so long as there is an efficient way of separating them from their wastes. When wars and natural catastrophes affect cities, disease often becomes a problem because water purification plants and sewage systems are damaged and stop working.

At a sewage treatment plant solids are separated from the rest of the sewage. Then the sewage is allowed to settle in sedimentation tanks. The wastes that settle on the bottom are pumped into settling beds where they dry out and are worked on by bacteria. The bacteria turn the wastes into a kind of compost which can be removed and used as a fertilizer on farmland.

In modern sewage treatment plants the liquid is sprayed over beds of gravel by using a sprinkler with rotary arms. A great mass of tiny plants and animals live on the surface of the gravel and feed on the nutrients in the liquid. Algae, bacteria, fungi, single-celled animals, and the larvae of certain types of flies all live on the gravel and break down the organic matter in the liquid and make it harmless. Birds such as swifts and swallows that catch flying insects are attracted to the gravel beds.

Sometimes sludge is pumped into ponds, which then soon become rich feeding grounds for many kinds of insects that can breed in the muddy pools. The insects become food for insect-eating birds, which land on the surface of the sludge as it dries out. The pied wagtail is a common bird around European sludge beds. In the winter, birds that have bred on the northern moors and Arctic tundra, such as snipe and dunlin, are common visitors.

Many cities are looking at ways of making use of sewage. Some cities have created wetlands so that sewage water can be used to benefit wildlife. In Arcata, California, the town has improved a marshland that is next to a sewage treatment plant. The marshland was dug out to create different levels over which water would circulate. Partly treated liquid sewage is then pumped into the marshland, where it provides nutrients for bacteria and plants. These in turn are food for animals. Peregrines falcons visit this sanctuary, and migrating ducks, terns, and waders stop off on their flight between their wintering grounds and their summer nesting habitats. Not only is a rich wildlife habitat created but the sewage water is also purified.

▽ The snipe is a wader with a long bill.

In hot water

All modern cities depend upon electricity. Electricity can be produced in several ways but the most common way is still to burn fossil fuels, such as coal, oil and natural gas, or to use nuclear fuels, to produce steam to drive the turbines of electricity generators. Cold water is used to condense the exhaust steam from the turbines. The water used for cooling picks up heat as the steam condenses into water. The outfall sites, where the cooling water is released into rivers or the sea are, therefore, sites of concentrated heat energy.

The warm water increases the growth of water plants. In temperate climates, the water is soon choked with plants and fish die from lack of oxygen. This process is often called thermal pollution. But in

△ The area around this power station, in Queensland, Australia, has been carefully landscaped to create a recreation area. It now attracts wildlife and tourists alike. The warm water outfall fills a lake, which was once a quarry, and provides a large area of constantly warm water for plants and animals. Some of the species that move into the new habitat, such as pelicans, are not normally found in the area.

countries with long, hard winters the warm water from power station outfalls benefits wildlife by keeping parts of rivers ice-free all through the year. These ice-free areas are then used by waterfowl. At Regina in Saskatchewan, the city has developed a nature reserve around its power station outfall.

The rewards of garbage

△ Many kinds of birds feed on garbage dumps.

Garbage dumps are usually found on the outskirts of towns and cities, usually on land that is not suitable for building or farming. Garbage dumps have their own food chains and succession of wildlife. The refuse is usually dumped in shallow layers and covered with soil. Many scavenging animals live on or visit garbage dumps. Rats, mice, crows, starlings, and many kinds of invertebrates search for discarded food or other organic material that they can eat. Hawks and owls hunt over dumps for rodents such as rats and mice. Sparrows, flycatchers, and wagtails hunt for insects and other invertebrates. One hundred years ago it was rare for sea gulls to live in towns. Today, they are among the most numerous birds on garbage dumps, where they feed on food waste and insects.

Garbage dumps also attract flocks of black kites, large birds of prey that are common in Africa, the Middle East, and Australia. They feed by scavenging and by hunting rodents, flying termites, and other small animals. Black kites were numerous in London up to the end of the eighteenth century. They played a very useful role in cleaning the capital at a time when people threw all their garbage and trash into the streets. Food residues, paper, cloth, wool, cotton, and other kinds of organic matter are food for fungi, bacteria, and small invertebrates such as springtail insects. By feeding on the waste they break it down into nutrients that are reusable by plants.

Bears on the prowl

Polar bears are annual visitors to the town of Churchill, on the western side of Hudson Bay in Canada, for about three months of the year. The town lies on a migration route for the bears. During the summer months the ice melts in the bay and the bears are forced ashore. Once ashore they are unable to hunt seals and they have to either fast or eat what comes their way. The town garbage dump has become a favorite attraction for them.

▷ A polar bear searches a garbage dump for food.

Compost

The compost heap found in many gardens is a kind of miniature high-energy habitat. The compost heap is the place where garden litter, mostly leaves and dead flowers, is put to rot down into compost, usually together with some household waste such as vegetable peelings and eggshells. The compost heap is, therefore, an accumulation of organic matter, just as the sewage treatment plant and garbage dump are. Within the heap, fungi and small animals such as worms and springtail insects find the garbage a rich source of food. Bacteria complete the breakdown of organic material into compost and the breakdown releases heat. Snakes lay their eggs in compost heaps to take advantage of the warmth. In Europe, the warmth also attracts creatures such as hedgehogs and slow worms (not a worm at all but a kind of reptile). These animals often escape the winter cold in the compost heap.

▽ Foxes have become quite common in some urban areas of Europe. They are attracted by the endless supply of food scraps.

Grasslands and the woodland edge

Most cities develop on land that has already been cleared in the past for farming. For wildlife the change from forests to farmland means a change from a multilayered, forest habitat to a single-layered field habitat. Birds of the forest canopy, such as warblers, are replaced by grassland birds, such as partridges. The replacement of farmland by suburbs is, for wildlife, a change back to something similar to woodland.

Town and city suburbs, especially spacious leafy ones, are woodland-edge habitats spread out over huge areas in some countries. Despite all the buildings and roads, about one third of most cities is still covered by some kind of vegetation. The natural woodland edge has features of both woodland and open habitats such as grassland. It is much the same in the suburban woodland edge. The lines of trees in streets, the trees in backyards and parks are the woodland element, while the grassy areas in cemeteries, parks, athletic fields, and lawns are the grassland element. Grassland is the habitat for several species of birds that are very rarely found in woodland, so areas of grassland mixed in with areas of trees can increase the total variety of wildlife living in a region.

In the churchyards

Churchyards and cemeteries are often islands of greenery in the built-up landscape. In Europe some churchyards and cemeteries have existed for centuries and over the years have become colonized by many kinds of plants, including those that take many years to become established such as cowslips, field woodrush, and doves foot cranesbill.

Churchyards can offer several different habitats. The headstones on the graves are usually made of limestone, which produces an alkaline habitat favored by many lichens. Rain washes lime into the soil nearby, where it makes the soil rich in calcium in which many plants usually found only in limestone country are able to live. They include spurge, wood anemone, and cow vetch.

In western Europe churches are often roosting places for bats, and barn owls and jackdaws may nest in the spires. Colonies of rooks may nest in old churchyards with tall trees of elm or beech. In summer the insects living in the grassy parts of the churchyards attract many kinds of insect-eating animals. Swifts and sand martins hawk for flying insects, while wagtails and wrens pick them off the ground and bushes. In the autumn wood pigeons search for acorns and ivy berries, while field fares and redwings— winter visitors from northern Europe—feed on the red holly berries.

Churchyards and cemeteries have had one

▽ Cemeteries in city centers can provide a haven for wildlife.

△ Barn owls nest in old buildings, church towers, and hollow trees.

surprising, but dramatic effect on the city environment. In the early part of the nineteenth century they were some of the best places for Sunday afternoon picnics for people living in towns, a custom that was particularly common in the rapidly growing cities of the northeastern United States. The obvious benefits for people of having pleasant, green places in which they could relax led to the movement to establish large parks in American cities.

One of the cities best known for its cemeteries rich in wildlife is Boston, Massachusetts. About one third of the open space in the city is found in its cemeteries.

The best example is the Mount Auburn Cemetery, which was laid out in the 1830s as the first garden cemetery in the United States. The cemetery has lots of woods and several ponds. Animals such as garter snakes, painted turtles, dusky salamanders, bullfrogs, and pickerel frogs are found there, together with over 90 species of birds. One reason this cemetery is rich in wildlife species is that it is next to a river, the Charles River. So the cemetery is not an isolated island surrounded by the built-up areas of Boston but a peninsula jutting out from the wildlife corridor that runs along the river.

On the athletic field

The mown grass of most athletic fields is not a particularly valuable wildlife habitat, although earthworms, grubs, and other invertebrates do attract birds such as starlings, European blackbirds, and rooks.

Golf courses are much better as a wildlife habitat. Birds such as linnets and yellowhammers live in the scrub between the fairways. Many golf courses are found on well-drained soils such as chalk or sands and these produce very fine turfs. The dry, short grasslands are good habitats for wild flowers such as wild campanula and orchids, and these flowers in turn attract many kinds of insects, particularly butterflies and bees. Golf courses also attract some surprising visitors: In Canberra, Australia, gray kangaroos leave the protection of the adjoining woodland to feed on the fairways on the Royal Golf Course, and in the United States, alligators sometimes move out of the swamps in the Florida Everglades onto nearby golf courses and lawns.

In praise of natural parks

During the nineteenth century a great effort was made by city governments to establish parks as pleasant places where people could relax. Parks are deliberate attempts to create

◁ Yellowhammer ▽ Central Park, New York

△ A border of wildflowers in a park in Amsterdam, Holland

artificial packages of countryside inside the towns. Some cities, especially in Europe, were lucky to have inherited large areas of open space set aside by kings as hunting forests in medieval times. In London, Hyde Park and Regent's Park are close to the center of the city and have a rich variety of woodland wildlife, particularly birds. In North America most cities had to create their parks from the land that was spared from the rapid pace of development. By the 1860s New York was establishing Central Park, one of the most ambitious attempts ever to design a natural landscape in a city.

Central Park is 840 acres of green open space crossed by paths and dotted with lakes. It was designed and promoted by Frederick Olmsted. His idea was to re-create the countryside in the city, so that people could relax away from the noise of the streets nearby. Many other cities in the United States have followed New York's lead; the five largest U.S. cities have over 338,000 acres of parks.

In the past, many city parks have been managed in a very formal way with neat flower beds, pruned shrubs, and closely mown grass. This kind of park management reduces the opportunities for wild plants and animals. However, more parks are now being managed to encourage wildlife. For example, waiting until late spring to mow grass allows wild plants to flower and set seed. This helps nectar-feeding insects and seed-eating animals. It also cuts down the cost of mowing.

The Dutch have created wild woodland parks in the heart of some of their cities. They have allowed the land between new apartment buildings to develop more or less naturally into woodland, with a little help from humans. Sand is added to the soil and mixtures of grasses are sown. Seeds of native trees such as birch, alder, and hawthorn are also sown, but once trees start to grow very little else is done. Natural areas like these are much richer in insects and birds than neatly tended parks.

Backyard wildlife

In the United States, Britain, Australia, and many other countries, most houses have yards of some kind. In Britain eight houses out of ten have yards, and their total area is greater than that of the country's nature reserves. In Germany, about six houses out of ten have yards; in Sweden only about four houses in ten have yards, but the grounds are usually much wilder than those in Britain or Germany and are very similar to the natural habitats found in the countryside.

The grounds of most houses are a patchwork of several habitats. Lawns are small areas of grassland. Bushes and hedges are patches of shrub woodland. Tall, mature trees are woodland edge habitat. The local vegetation attracts a variety of birds. Nuthatches and tree creepers hunt for insects living between the pieces of bark on tree trunks, great tits search on the ground among the fallen leaves and twigs while blue tits hunt for insects in the tree crowns. The grounds also provide many of these birds with a place to nest. Holes in large trees provide nesting cavities for tawny owls and in America they are used by raccoons (see also page 18). In large old places it may even be possible for birds that need a lot of space, such as the sparrow hawk, to hunt. The sparrow hawk has been seen swooping upon sparrows in large grounds. The carrion crow is a dominant bird of suburban areas where it roosts in large trees. Its relative the rook, on the other hand, very rarely comes into towns and cities.

In some places large animals will visit suburban backyards. Foxes are common in parts of Bristol and London in England, and coyotes live in the suburban gullies of Los Angeles in the United States. In England muntjac deer are known to visit gardens to eat rose leaves, and in North America where yards and gardens adjoin areas of woodland whitetail deer are visitors.

Garden ponds provide a plentiful source of water for animals living in and visiting the area. Many birds also like to bathe as well as to drink and some species, such as house martins, need mud to make their nests. Ponds are also mini wetland habitats. Algae

△ A garden pond attracts wildlife.

and other water plants are food and shelter for small animals such as water fleas, which in turn are food for water insects, small fish, and birds. Sometimes herons and other large water birds will visit garden ponds, although pond owners with ornamental fish usually resent their visits.

Too much tidiness in a garden is a problem for wildlife. A piece of ground left uncultivated will soon be invaded by plants

▽ These white-tailed fawns are two weeks old.

that many people call weeds. But a weed is merely a plant growing where we do not want it. Some very common weeds are extremely valuable to certain kinds of wild animals. Nettles, for example, are the chief food for the caterpillars of red admiral, peacock, and small tortoiseshell butterflies. Thistles and groundsel produce small seeds eaten by seed-eating birds such as goldfinches. The gardener benefits from such wildlife visits, too. A wren, for example, can eat 500 caterpillars and aphids in a day, so garden pests can be controlled naturally if part of a garden is allowed to grow wild.

Monkey tricks

The vervet monkey is naturally an animal of the African savannas and woodland edge. It sleeps in trees and uses them to escape from predators, although it is adapted to search for food in open country and can climb, jump, and also swim very well. It eats a wide variety of leaves, fruits, seeds, and insects, as well as lizards and birds' eggs and young. Leafy tropical gardens suit vervet monkeys because of the mixture of foods and the shelter provided by garden trees and shrubs.

Rhesus macaque monkeys are found in northern India. The rhesus macaques have adapted to life in gardens, yards and

△ A vervet monkey feeding on fruit

orchards. They eat grains, fruits, seeds, roots, and small animals. In the state of Uttar Pradesh one third of the state's monkeys live in cities. In fact, more monkeys live in cities in India than in forests.

A backyard classic

The European blackbird is naturally a bird of open deciduous woodland with a rich layer of fallen leaves and humus, in which the birds can search for food. As the suburbs of cities have expanded during this century the blackbird has become the classic backyard bird. Well-watered lawns provide a rich supply of earthworms, while snails and insects are to be found in the flower beds. Leafy bushes and garden hedges also provide ample nesting habitat. Blackbirds are also helped by people who put food out for birds during the winter. By adapting so well to suburbs, blackbirds are probably more numerous now than they have ever been.

New landscapes, new opportunities

Going green

Are there ways of improving our cities as places for desirable kinds of wildlife as well as making them better places for people? The answer is almost certainly yes, and although no city has all the answers there are many examples in cities around the world that show what is possible. Increasing the amount and variety of natural vegetation is the key.

Cities are warmer than the surrounding countryside because of the nature of building materials and because energy is used for heating and air conditioning (see page 6). In warm climates cities can become uncomfortably hot because of the "heat island" effect. However, vegetation, particularly trees, makes the climate cooler because plants transpire water vapor during the day, which cools the air. Trees are natural air conditioners. So belts of trees reaching into the heart of cities will improve the climate and provide habitat for wildlife, particularly insects and insect-eating birds. Trees, especially those with large leaves, also trap some of the particles of soot and dust in the air and help to clean the air we breathe. Trees and shrubs make city centers and suburbs quieter places by absorbing noise produced by traffic.

Town trees

Nearly two thirds of the trees planted along London's streets are London plane trees. This species has been planted so much because it is able to put up with a great deal of air pollution. The outer bark of plane trees is constantly peeling away. As the dirt-clogged outer bark is lost, the tree can "breathe" through the pores in the new bark underneath.

Plane trees use the wind to carry their pollen, so they do not provide nectar for insects or birds. But their large size and their dense summer foliage do allow squirrels and many kinds of birds to make their nests safe from human interference. The London plane is also the chief food plant of the vaporer moth caterpillars, which hatch into the tiny brown moths that are common in many of London's streets in the spring.

Lime trees are large spreading, deciduous trees. In some cities long avenues of lime trees have been planted for their beauty and the shade they provide. Many animals shelter and nest in their crowns, where they

▷ London plane trees have flaky bark (inset).

▽ Landscaping allows wildlife to live next to industry.

are safe from human disturbance.

In summer the leaves and shoots of the lime become infested with vast numbers of lime **aphids**, which feed on the sugar-rich sap produced by the leaves. The sap contains more sugar than the aphids can use and some passes through the aphids and forms what is called honeydew on the surface of the leaves. The honeydew is not wasted, since it is used by ants, flower flies and moths. The aphids also attract predators such as ladybugs, so there is a quite complex food chain based on the lime trees of city streets.

As a general rule, the variety of wildlife species increases as we move out from the built-up city centers to the less densely built-up suburbs. However, if there is natural vegetation many wild animals can live very close to our city centers. The old railroad station in Berlin (see page 23) shows how rich in wildlife a piece of wasteland can become without any deliberate help from people. We need to create habitats in which desirable animals can breed. By increasing the numbers of trees and shrubs the desirable animals may move in and compete with the undesirable animals. Besides having fewer pests, leafy suburbs are usually pleasanter places for people to live in than densely crowded ones.

City habitats are fragmented into patches, which can reduce the variety of wildlife species. The patches are richer in wildlife if they are linked to each other and to the surrounding countryside by corridors of natural vegetation. The Mount Auburn Cemetery in Boston (see page 35) shows how rich in birdlife a city reserve can be

▽ Trees and water in a park in Melbourne, Australia, create a pleasant environment for people and a habitat for wildlife.

when it is linked to a river corridor. An important part of making our cities better places for wildlife is to have areas of woodland and other types of natural habitat deep inside cities, with wide corridors of natural vegetation linking city centers to the countryside.

Wildlife helps to make each city feel different from others. Modern suburbs often look and feel the same wherever they are because of the design of the buildings and the materials of which they are made. But a hill with its own wood is not the same as any other hill. It has its own character, its own sense of place, which is important to the people who live there.

▽ Neat, weed-free flower borders are less attractive to wildlife than untidy, more natural planting.

△ Community forests and other conservation areas provide ideal sites for young people to study wildlife in their own city.

Community forests

The community forest is one of the most exciting ideas for improving the land around cities for wildlife and providing places for recreation. The principle is being developed in several countries in Europe, and in the United States urban forestry, a similar idea is increasing in importance. In England community forests are being planned to improve some of the large urban areas where there is a lot of derelict land lying unused. Much of south Staffordshire, in the north of England, has been scarred by mining and quarrying. It was one of the first areas in the world to become industrialized in the eighteenth century. The region became known as the Black Country because of the great quantities of smoke and dust that were produced by the factories and workshops. The whole region provides an opportunity to use the healing powers of nature to produce a greener landscape with a greater variety of wildlife habitats.

The idea is not to cover the area with thick forest but to create a good mixture of forest, meadows, and other wildlife habitats. The forests will be linked to the city parks, yards, gardens, and tree-lined streets by making use of riverbanks and river floodplains as wildlife corridors. By this means, the wildlife habitats in the cities will not be isolated from those in the countryside but will be peninsulas of vegetation jutting into the built-up landscape. People will be able to enjoy nature close to their homes and not just in places that can be visited only occasionally and at great expense. The forests will be used for activities such as walking, fishing, wildlife study, and orienteering, and local people will help to manage the forest.

Although nature left to itself will produce complex and diverse ecosystems we have to take an active part in managing nature if we want to use it to provide particular products and benefits. For example, trees can provide shade around houses but to get the best effect we have to choose certain kinds and plant them in the right place. If we want forests to produce fuel wood then we need quick-growing trees for periodic cutting. If we want forests with tawny owls then we must also have old trees with hollows. Managing nature is fun and the more people that can be involved the better. It is the best way of developing an understanding of nature and a feeling of harmony with it.

aphids—a group of small insects such as the greenfly that feed by sucking the juices of plants.

Large birds such as white storks (right) and herons (below) often nest in cities.

44

Index